Stuart Sterne

Beyond the Shadow

And Other Poems

Stuart Sterne

Beyond the Shadow
And Other Poems

ISBN/EAN: 9783744709712

Printed in Europe, USA, Canada, Australia, Japan

Cover: Foto ©Thomas Meinert / pixelio.de

More available books at **www.hansebooks.com**

Books by Stuart Sterne.

ANGELO. A Poem. 18mo, gilt top, $1.00.
GIORGIO, AND OTHER POEMS. 18mo, full gilt, $1.00.
BEYOND THE SHADOW. Poems. 18mo, $1.00.

HOUGHTON, MIFFLIN & CO.
BOSTON AND NEW YORK.

BEYOND THE SHADOW
AND OTHER POEMS

BY

STUART STERNE

BOSTON AND NEW YORK
HOUGHTON, MIFFLIN AND COMPANY
The Riverside Press, Cambridge
1888

Copyright, 1888,
By HOUGHTON, MIFFLIN & CO.

All rights reserved.

The Riverside Press, Cambridge:
Electrotyped and Printed by H. O. Houghton & Co.

To

ONE "BEYOND THE SHADOW"

THROUGH WHOM HAS COME TO ME

A HERITAGE OF TEARS, BUT ALSO A PURER FAITH IN GOD AND MAN,

AND A DEEPER COMPREHENSION OF

LIFE, DEATH, AND ETERNITY,

IN UNFALTERING LOVE ARE INSCRIBED

These Pages,

BY

S. S.

CONTENTS.

AFTER DEATH.
    I. A Voice from Above 7
    II. A Voice from Below 13
    III. The Voice from Above 19
    IV. Second Voice from Above 26
A Maiden's Question 37
Surrender 41
Yearning 43
A Flower of Hope 45
Insufficiency 48
Two Sonnets 50
The Face of God 52
A Well of Sorrow 54
Through the Midnight Sky 57
God's Peace 59
Hymn 61
Into Thy Hands 63
Sonnet 66
The Herb Forgetfulness 67
Thy Will be Done 69
My Father's Child 70

AFTER-YEARS	72
HOPE	77
CUPID	78
YOUNG LOVE	81
HIS WILL, NOT MINE	83
SHIPWRECKED	86
LOVE HAS DECEIVED ME	88
MARIANA	90
THE SILENT HOUSE	92
SONG	94
LOVE ME	95
SORROW	96
MEASURE FOR MEASURE	98
THE STROLLING PLAYER	103
THE OLD POET'S REST	105
DESIRE	106
TRUST ME NOT, LOVE	107
THY HEART IS LIKE THE SUN	109
WHERE HAST THOU GONE, O MY SOUL	110
SONNET	112
OH, BAR THY GATES	113
ROME	115
SUNDAY	118
TO AN UNKNOWN LOVE	119
O FLOWER MOST FINE	123
GREECE	125
LIKE TO A BROOK, O SONG	127
BE STILL	130
ALL FUTURE YEARS ALONG	132
ABOVE AND EARTH AND TIME	135
IN VAIN	137

CONTENTS.

Eternal Spring	140
Sonnet	142
Transformation	143
Sonnet	144
Two Sonnets. Solitude and Silence	145
Sonnet	147

BEYOND THE SHADOW.

AFTER DEATH.

I.

A VOICE FROM ABOVE.

Where am I? — Do I live? — When yesternight,
Even as the tide went out 'neath paling stars,
My fevered eyes closed wearily, I caught
In the last gleam of fading consciousness,
The whispered words, "'T is over, — he is dead!"
And yet, — oh strange! — these eyes are open now,
And painless lift their lids! — I gaze around, —
I turn my head, — I see and feel and touch
A hand, an arm, — beneath me trunk and limbs
More light, more fine, yet not all unlike those
That shall be laid away beneath the ground,
Which sometimes proved a burden, weighing down
The spirit with their cumbrance; yet more days

Filled me with a brave sense of joy and power,
When lustily, in full, free swing they sported
In the glad earthly sunshine.

And is this
That second better world, whereof so much
Was said and preached and sung to us below? —
This leaden, low-hung, murky sky, but cleft
By a dull bar of orange far beyond, —
This heaving, turbid sea, whose fretful waves
Chafe the bleak shore, and this gray, barren rock
Whereon I lie? — nude, without hope, alone, —
Even as ten thousand centuries ago
The first created man was helpless cast
On that rude nether world, whence but so late
I was translated hither.

Ah, look there!
A sight no living eye has ever seen! —
In the dim distance, their blurred outlines dark
Against that tawny bar across the sky,
A cloud of shadowy shapes, adrift, awhirl,
Like seething vapors lashed by wind and rain, —
Thousands on thousands, a vast, countless throng,
A shifting, writhing, mighty multitude
Of human forms that endless pass and pass!

AFTER DEATH.

Departed spirits like myself, past doubt,
And like myself, here, to their own surprise,
Clothed in some semblance of their earthly garb,
And finer substance.

                Ah, and hark! there rises,
Distinct from muttering sea and soughing wind,
A sound no living ear has ever heard, —
A weird, wild, wailing note, a long-drawn chant,
That comes in fitful gusts, swells, sinks and dies
In broken accents on the heavy air,
Waking faint echoes.

                Who, what were they all,
Those flitting shades? — how came they to this
      shore,
That lies like a bleak, desert, fire-swept island,
Sunless and starless, in the very midst
Of God's great universe of light and joy? —
God! — oh, tremendous word! — let me not now
Give without trembling utterance to the name
My heedless tongue was wont to take in vain! —
Who, what was I myself, — how came I here?

Let me remember! — Yes, I was a man,
Fair, tall, of powerful frame and lofty brow,

With eloquent lips that swayed the souls of men,
Persuading them to laughter or to tears,
And with a heart in this broad, deep-voiced
    breast
Full as the sunny grape of generous sweetness,
That should have proved a blessing to my kind.
God lavished on me rich, rare, happy gifts,
Opened a thousand opportunities
For goodness and for greatness! Oh, but I —
I, like a foolish boy, a ruthless knave,
Who plucks for wanton sport with impious hands
The fairest crimson heart of all the summer
To scatter its sweet petals to the wind;
I used, spoiled, wasted all, — squandered and
    spent, .
Within a few mad years, the garnered wealth
That should have served me through a long,
    glad life;
Passed the loud nights 'mid laughter, wine, and
    song,
And kisses from red lips, bought for a price, —
The days in idle pleasure, nothing, — not
My children's voices, nor their baby hands,
Could win or pluck me from. My children, — ay,
For God made me a father!

AFTER DEATH.

                            So at last
The soul that drank too thirstily and deep
Of all the bitter sweetness of the world,
Forgot all else, and from the fevered brain
There faded like poor, pallid smoke, high thought
And lofty purpose and immortal aim;—
Nay, do not smile; for I, too, knew them once,
High thought and lofty purpose, even I,—
Like some dim gleaming castle in the clouds,
A child may feebly reach for.

                            So at last
I shrank to but a shadow of myself,
The strength of manhood shriveled in my veins,
The very heart itself, grown tainted too,
Contracted and turned crabbed, harsh, and sour,
Even as the generous juices of the grape
May rot through some unsoundness in the vine,
For something from the very first beginning
Must needs have been amiss, when I was made,
Some mortal weakness lurking in the blood,
Else, mayhap, had I not gone thus astray,
So far, so hopelessly!— And like a tower
Sapped at the root from its foundation stone,
I crumbled, tottered, then gave way and fell;—
I who so gayly rode life's awful sea,

But like a summer bark with silken sails,
Thoughtless of all the storms that sleep below,
Was shipwrecked utterly!—perished long ere
That brief, last mortal weakness stole upon me,
And men said, "He is dead!"

                        And now, what now?
Even here alone, on this dark, desert shore
Of a dim, unknown, strange, and awful world,
Cut off from all companionship, all ties
Of love and comfort, I must undertake
A sore, tremendous, never-ending task,—
The slow salvation of my soul! Ay, from
Such scant material, such few broken spars
As I may find in that abandoned soul,
Build me a new, nobler, more worthy life
Than ever yet it dreamed.

                        Yet where begin,
How set to work? Ah, how, save but with Him,
Him the beginning and the end of all things
Of earth or heaven! Behold, I move, I rise,
I stand erect and firm! But joyfully
Do my repentant knees and humbled brow
Sink back again to kiss the barren ground!—
All-merciful, Almighty, Infinite God,

Whom in the world below I never knew,
Turn not Thy face from me, — my first act here
Is prostrate to adore Thy Blessed Name!

II.

A VOICE FROM BELOW.

Hast thou in truth passed to that shore we call
The land of darkness and eternal silence?
Thou too, whom our fond hearts were wont to
    think
So panoplied in fairest life and power,
That mortal ills could scarce assail thee? — Ay,
Gone mutely, with veiled head? — Thou, on whose
    lips
Sat golden speech like music, and a smile
So infinite sweet, that with its fading out
Something was taken from the sunlight, never
To be restored, and one gray shadow more
Added to weary earth.

                  Here, in this world,
While thy gay heart still basked in light and joy,
My eager soul was wont to follow thee
With love and yearning. — It was with thee oft

At noisy feast and revel, or again
In those rare lonely hours of silent night,
When it may be thy nobler nature woke
To warn and plead aloud. — And so even now
It would go forth, groping its fearless way
'Mid the dim shadows of that shore of death,
To pierce the mystery and awful gloom
That wrap thee round, — be with thee still
    through all
The sore probation that must now be thine,
Yes, by the laws of everlasting justice,
Thy daily cup!

              For God had made thee great,
As rich in substance and most precious seed,
As some proud tree, whose heart shuts in the
    promise
Of thousand fragrant flowers and golden fruit,
And yet thou wast but small, thy barren life
In the few sickly blossoms it put forth,
But half fulfilling the immortal bond,
For thine own heedless hand marred wantonly
God's image in thy soul, until at last
That very soul itself, long sapped, gave way,
Bore down with it, in its tremendous fall,
Thy noble frame, still green in years and honors.

And yet, — oh thought of helpless anguish! — yet
It had not been impossible to save thee,
Yes, oh sweet stars, save thee for earth and
    heaven!
Love might have saved thee, — woman's love, —
    a love —
— Oh let me dare to utter it! — like mine,
The deepest, purest thou hadst ever known!
A love God knows, that did not ask for much
Save but the highest boon, — to serve and cherish
All that was best within thee, minister
To thy most noble needs and loftiest aims,
Fan into life and nourish with its breath
The all too feebly flickering, sacred fire
Upon thy altar, — sunk to ashes now,
Where lies the shrine in ruins!

                      Aye, I loved thee,
And thou hadst guessed it, for I never hid
My heart from thee, brave in its innocence,
And though thou daredst not wholly take that
    heart,
Yet couldst thou not reject it utterly,
For some fine instinct whispered to thy soul
Thy sorest need, thy last undying hope,
Was in such love as this. — Once, I remember,

Hearing of it thy ready tears gushed forth,
And oft I know it moved thee to perceive
My ceaseless, tender thought of thee, and some-
    times
I ween my trembling fingers found and struck
The deepest chords thy breast had left, yet oh,
Even those so faint they brought my aching heart
No more content than one poor drop of water
To burning lips long parched with fevered
    thirst ! —
Such were my dearest joys ! Without avail
Would my great love have folded round thy life
Strong sheltering arms to keep thee from all ill ;
Without avail my soul reached out for thine
To purify, make new, — in vain, in vain,
The effort hopeless, yet divine ! — What power,
What very god transformed a hollow ring
To a deep golden goblet, that may hold
Unspilled the choicest vintage of our lives,
A glistening pebble to a granite rock,
On whose eternal basis we may found
Our soul's salvation ? —

               And long-suffering love,
That had endured unnumbered, nameless pangs,
Been baffled, bruised, struck to the heart of
    hearts

AFTER DEATH.

A thousand times, and yet a thousand times
As by a miracle won back to life, —
Sickened at last, and died in sorest travail,
Forever and past hope! — so utterly,
That when I met thy dim, unconscious gaze
On the last couch that bore thy weary frame, —
When all was over, and I knew the lips
That mine had kissed, rigid in death, — no cry
Sprang to these lips, wellnigh as set as thine,
No tears to these dry eyes, drained long ago,
And in the stony silence of the heart
That had so freely spilled its ruddy life,
Naught woke or stirred, save but the feeble voice
Of a large, general pity!

                           And what now? —
Must I surrender thee, thy stricken soul,
To the chill love and prayers and tears of her
Who bore thy name, but to thy heart was dead,
Or to that other, not thy wife, and yet
The mother of thy best beloved child?
To any one, who, in the garish sunlight,
E'er quaffed with thee the sparkling draft of joy?
No, by great Heaven, all that is done forever!
Those voiceless shadows of the vanished past
Fall back and fade from sight and leave thee
    free,

All those false ties are snapped, have dropped away
Even with thy earthly frame! — Now, now at last
Am I thy sole companion, — I, O God,
Who never knew but love's most bitter cup! —
Now, 'mid dread darkness and unbroken gloom,
I claim the place beside thee, that I won
In untold anguish, — claim it now in joy!
For something still, despite this double death
Of life in thee, of love in me, something
That cannot perish while my soul survives,
Knits me to thee! —

    Yet stay, — what do I dream, —
It may not be! — E'en I must stand aside,
Thyself alone must work thine own salvation,
Thou under God's dear mercy! — Ay, to His
Relentless justice, yet unfailing love,
Into His chastening, yet most tender Hands,
Do I commit thy soul, and am content,
What though from out these barren eyes once more
The blinding tears gush forth, my friend, my lover!

III.

THE VOICE FROM ABOVE.

How long I have been here, what months, what years,
— Or can it be but many nights and days? —
What time has passed, since I first woke from death
And wondering found myself on this bleak shore,
I may not say, — or if they count it time,
Or if they call it day or night at all,
This endless interchange of pallid dawn
And dusky twilight, and dim shifting dark
That never broadens into noon nor deepens
To golden sunset or a star-filled night.
Methinks a hundred thousand days like this
Have risen, died, come again, slow, weary, hopeless,
Amid my solitude, crept by at last,
Though how, I know not. — Only this I know,
That even as in the ground shut far away
From sun and star, there lies some quickening seed
Which hourly swells and throbs with fuller life,
Puts forth a delicate root — a tender germ —

The promise of a leaf, till round about
The very earth that held it captive long,
Thrills as with joy and parts to set it free, —
So do I bear in this dark breast of mine
Unfolding more and more from day to day
The consciousness, the thought, the love of God,
Thrice blessed be His Name!

                           And now and then
There slowly filters through this dusk a whiteness
Not day, but like a broken gleam of day
Before its fading, and around me steals
A breath of faint, sweet perfume, passing grateful
Even as the voiceless presence of a friend,
Even as the prayers and tears and loving thought
Of some most tender, faithful heart! Yet whose?
None lives that here would follow such as me!
A subtle essence, strange and yet familiar,
That sometime, somewhere on the earth below
Methinks my grosser senses must have known
And yet but half received. — But when and how?
Surely amid no feast and revel, surely
From none of those, — oh memories forlorn!
Who in a wanton hour of mad delight
These arms have clasped, these lips, — yet no,
    thank God!

Not these: I was made new!—Stay, let me think,
Strive to remember,—was there no one else?
One who perchance,—yes, yes,—ah, Heaven,
    'tis that—
I know thee now, sweet spirit!—It is thou,
My dearest, best of friends, my little woman,
Who send'st this message of brave cheer and hope,
Whose soul would seek and follow me even here,
Amid the shades of death!—oh joy supreme,
I never dared to dream myself so blest,
Thy heart, I feared, had cast me off forever!

She was not passing fair, mayhap, nor yet
In the first flush of youth,—a fleeting glance
Might not have turned to gaze at her again,
But mine soon learned to dwell with secret joy
Upon that noble face.—Her brow was thoughtful,
And from the quiet, dark brown eyes looked
    forth
A soul most honest, earnest, deep and tender,
A virgin soul as pure as childhood's self,
Untouched by all the evils of the world,
A soul God blessed with power to read the truth,
Simple in all her ways, of gentle speech,
—Ay, from the serious lips there ever came
A low sweet voice and sometimes pleasant laugh-
    ter,—

Brave, patient, generous, she revealed herself
A spirit rare and high, of such fine mould,
So far above all other creatures made
In woman's image, that had crossed my path,
So far, alas! above my wretched self,
That all too long my dull, corrupted sense
Scarce marked her from the crowd.

      How first, and when,
She came still as a star, into my life,
I do not well remember, but methinks
'T was for some noble purpose of my art,
Wherein her heart was bound, like mine. And
  after
Many a long hour, — oh golden memories,
Of those glad, unforgotten days of earth! —
We spent in earnest talk, I smiling sometimes,
In my sad earthly wisdom wont to call
Her aim too lofty and her flight too high,
Though now I know, sweet Saint, that by those
  laws
Thy deeper insight strove to teach me then,
The world, God's world, is ruled, must stand or
  fall!
That her great soul was ever drawn to mine,
A rushlight glimmering feebly through the dark,

Beside her own, no more, — was passing strange,
But that she gave me too, — let me dare speak,
What she was not unwilling I should guess! —
That stainless gem above all price, her heart, —
Me, a poor creature smirched with many sins,
Seemed God's own miracle! — I wept hot tears
When first I learned it, — tears of wondering pity,
Of fear, of joy, for her, for me, us both,
And once, twice, thrice, — yes, at three different times,
She put her modest arms about my neck,
And her sweet lips to mine. — She knew most well
I could not claim her, though not all dark ties
That held me bound, and yet God's purest angels,
While the dim earth has stood with Heaven above,
Recorded not a holier kiss than that
On our sad wedded lips! — The heavy heart
To which I clasped thee, little woman, thrilled
With sudden, unknown hope, — for one brief hour
It seemed that touch had purged me from all taint,
Sin dropped away, I walked a new-made man,
Redeemed, blest, sanctified! — But, oh, God help me!

Even then I sank again: the thought of thee,
Thy voice, thy face, drowned in wild pleasure's
    tide,
Forgot the benediction of thy lips
Amid accursed kisses! Ay, past doubt,
A thousand times some coarser strain in me
Jarred rudely on thy soul,—yes, now and then,
I caught a troubled shadow in thine eyes!—
Until thy delicate spirit must have turned
In loathing from the bitter cup whereof
It drained so deep a draught!

                          And yet for all,
She never wholly knew, nor I confessed,
How dear, how precious, what a blessed part
Of all my deepest life, she grew to be,
How all my nobler nature clave to her
With strong and stronger tendrils.—'Mid the
    throng
Of eager, upturned faces wont to greet me
Night after night,—for I was one of those
Who on the stage which mimics life, show forth
The passions and the pains and joys of men,—
It was her eyes I sought and loved to find
With their still, earnest gaze, that marked, I
    knew,

Each lofty effort and each finer touch, —
Her praise and very blame I loved to hear
Better than hollow thunders of applause
Too easily won. — In lonely hours, her face
Oft rose before me, sweet yet sorrowful,
And sometimes suddenly filled me with a strange
Unutterable yearning, sharp as death,
And when I broke, and to my puzzled brain
The strands of life grew tangled hopelessly,
All the bleak world transformed to shifting chaos,
Where my dim vision strained to grasp and hold
Some distinct form, some gleam of steady light, —
— It was her image that stood clearly out,
Pure, radiant, beautiful, from all that maze
Of never-lifting cloud. —

       And now, and now, —
What though I trembling thought that all was
 ended
Forever, — yet she comes to me again, —
Oh, Heaven, what may I hope, what glean there-
 from?
That still, — that she even now —

       My God, my Father!
If in Thy infinite mercy Thou wilt deign

To hearken to the humblest of Thy children,
Receive a prayer wrung from the deepest heart
Of him whom now no earthly passion moves, —
— Upon my bended knees I here implore Thee,
If it be possible somehow, sometime,
In the long course of all eternity,
That I grow less unworthy, — I will wait
And hope and serve with never-failing patience, —
Oh, mayhap in a thousand, thousand years,
My God, my Father, — give her then to me!

IV.

SECOND VOICE FROM ABOVE.

Ay, let us pause here for a while, Sweet Soul,
Upon this gentle hill 'neath spreading trees,
Where towards the left lie the wide happy
    fields,
Flushed with the mellow light of evening now,
Skirting the wood, o'er whose dim golden path
Our Loves shall come to us, — and on the right
We may look upward, downward, everywhere
Into immeasurable crystal space!
— Yes, this is well; sit here with thy dear hand
Close clasped in mine!

                        See where, far, far below,
Floats like a tiny, troubled cloud the earth,
The poor, bleak earth, our former home! Oh, sometimes
Even here, in all this infinite content,
A nameless pity seizes on my heart
For those who still 'mid doubt and fear and darkness
Grope their blind pathway through that vale of tears!
And yet God lives to them, even as He lived
To thee, to me, — the same Immortal Hope
He ever proved since earth came from His hands,
To all who, rising over death triumphant,
Have entered here at last! —

                        Friend, thou hast prayed me
Sometime to tell thee of myself, of how
I lost and won my Love — him who next God
Makes Heaven to me, and everlasting life!
I will so now, — the memories of earth
Are strong upon me, — tell thee all, but yet
Briefly as may be! — 'T is a sad, dark tale,
Oh, infinite darker, sadder than thine own,
Indeed, indeed, though thou look'st up at me
With gentle wonder in thy happy eyes!

When thy dear Love died for his country's weal,
Struck by a shot that slew two lives in one,
Thou as thy heart broke, gazing on the face
That smiled no more, hadst yet one drop of joy,
Exceeding joy, in thy most bitter cup, —
Your mutual, holy, pure and single love,
The thought his stainless soul went straight to God,
Thy image there undimmed, the parting breath
Upon his lips, thy name! — But I, but I
Lived and loved on, knowing that he I loved
Was all unworthy of my love, as men
Had blindly said, though God judged otherwise, —
That stifling nobler promptings, he had fallen
From honor and high virtue countless times, —
That having wife and child his arms had clasped
— God wot how oft! — fair other forms, his lips
Kissed other lips than theirs. in wanton hours
Of idle pleasure! — Oh, yet let me pause,
Enough, enough! — Spare me from telling further
What but to think on hurts! —
                                    I knew all this,
And shrank from him, — scorned, pitied, judged, condemned,
Yet loved him still! — This was my sin, perchance,

And if it was, O God, I paid its price
In tears of blood! —

     Nay, Friend, let not thy heart
Be over-troubled, nor thy brow grow dark!
Pray clearly understand it was not thus
When first I saw him! — then I knew of naught,
Not even he was wed. — Ay, poor, pale Shade
Who bore his name, yet to his heart was dead
Long years before he looked upon my face,
Thou know'st I never wronged thee, 't was not I
Who won his soul from thee! I loved not him,
— Or so I thought at first, — who loved not me,
— Nay, I am sure, nor then nor till long after!
But his great art, I fancied, drew my heart
With power resistless, and too boldly brave,
I blindly followed till it was too late,
Till I had drained again and yet again
The poisoned cup that proved so deadly sweet,
Till my poor soul was hopeless knit with his
For all eternity! —

     Long, long, I tell thee,
I never knew but all was well with him,
Fondly believing that it must be so.
For something in his voice and eye and smile,

The grave and yet most gracious presence, full
Of generous sweetness and mild warmth and
    light,
For these alone I ever found in him, —
Even as an autumn day of golden sunshine,
Though sometimes dashed, to eyes as keen as
    mine,
With sudden sadness. — Ay, all, all, I say,
Seemed to make answer to a secret question : —
Whatever pangs and bitterness life brought,
His heart is stainless, and his mind attuned
To lofty purpose, — into his dear keeping
Would I entrust my own immortal soul!
— Nor did I wholly err! — For oh, in truth,
He was most nobly, richly, greatly planned,
Full of the seeds of all divinest things,
His deepest wrong to be too easily won
From the fair heights he clearly saw above,
To low and lower levels, till, methinks
His better angel must have wept beholding
The radiant image of the Lord he knew
And yet denied, trailed through the common
    dust!

But late I say, and by most slow degrees,
The knowledge and conviction that in him,

AFTER DEATH.

Him too, there dwelled a taint of odious sin,
Broke on my doubting spirit, which believed
And hoped in him, past evidence and proof.
But when they came, and I could doubt no longer,
Oh God, what tempests and wild bursts of tears,
What hours of anguish and heart-broken prayer,
What travail of the spirit, gasping, stifling
For light and air, amid unbroken night,
Till reason like a feebly flickering torch
Wind-blown and rain-drenched, seemed nigh spent, sometimes!
If it be true we must to Hell descend
Ere we may after find the path to Heaven,
I drank its bitter, maddening waters then,—
— If once within the lives of all there comes
A Passion, in some humble way recalling
The pangs of Him who suffered on the Cross,
That was my Calvary!—

                Nay, nay, Sweet Soul,
Thou say'st I'm white and tremble, and I feel
Thy loving arms steal round me tenderly!
'T is strange mayhap, these memories of old
Should have such power to shake me thus even now!

— But think upon some gentle fawn, hedged in
By forest fires, whose cruel tongues of flame
Do merciless scorch and gnaw its tender vitals,
Till blinded, breathless, mad with writhing pangs,
It turns and turns again to find escape,
And meets but blazing death on every hand! —
— Or on a new-fledged bird, his delicate breast
Transfixed by some fierce thorn, that as in vain
He fluttering, bleeding, strives to break away,
Pierces but deeper through the quivering flesh, —
And thou may'st guess, perchance — Yet no, no,
    no!
All these have but the sting of outward pain,
No sense of subtler and more awful anguish,
No image but itself can serve to show
The aching, bleeding, bursting heart, the tortures
Of the despairing soul wellnigh undone,
Struck in its deepest and most sacred life,
By touching evil! — Of a soul born white
By Heaven's dear grace, and loathing unclean
    things,
Yet sickening 'neath the thought, — mayhap I,
    too,
Shall perish now, shall be attainted, smirched,
Till God Himself shall turn His Face from me,
Through love of him who turned from God!
    And yet,

For all and all, through hell and death and darkness,
Distracted, shuddering, shrinking, still compelled
To follow and to love! — Oh, Sweetest Soul,
Believe me, oh believe me, who through him
Wellnigh myself have known its mortal pangs,
There is no ill, no loss, no death, save sin!

Yet is 't not written, Love shall conquer Death,
Ay, even the death of deaths? — So love lived on,
Dwelled with me still, an hourly agony,
As Saints of old 't is said were wont to wear
A belt of chafing nettles next their heart, —
Lived on despite of thousand wounds it suffered,
Though at each fierce, unworthy stab I thought —
This is the end! — Now, now it bleeds to death,
And so most well! — Or it or I must perish!
A hundred times I deemed the victory mine,
Believed that all indeed for aye was over,
Oh but to find myself a hundred times
Deceived in that most hopeless, vain conceit! —
Again and yet again with twofold force,
With new-found life, triumphantly it rose,
Even like a spring long flowing underground
Bursts forth at last past human power to stay,
Like that charmed tree from whose immortal trunk

For one poor twig lopped off, sprang twenty branches
In richest leaf and flower.

                          And thus indeed,
The end drew nigh, — nay, not of love to me,
But life to him, still green in years and honors.
The end yet the beginning; for from death,
What has been called so with most ill a title,
Sprang new, immortal life to both of us.
To him redemption came; to me, when earth
Had closed above his head, deep, infinite peace
In the blest thought — Whatever now betide,
He is with God! — no longer tossed and fretted
'Mid the fierce heats of the tumultuous world
That all too easily lured and conquered him!
And then with nameless joy broke on my heart,
Like a slow, radiant dawn, the consciousness, —
He lives, I love him, oh and under God,
My love may help him in the sore probation,
That by all laws of everlasting justice
Must now be his! — Help him I know not how,
Yet God's dear mercy does, — He will dispose!

Thus patiently, at peace, and full of hope,
I lingered on the earth, whose sun had fled,
For ten years more. — To him he says they were

AFTER DEATH.

As twenty thousand, while in gloomy twilight,
'Mid pangs unspeakable, he toiled alone
At that tremendous, never-ending task,
The saving of his soul, — but faint of heart,
And nigh despairing sometimes, yet sustained
To feel how slowly, surely, day by day,
God's image ever grew within that soul,
And by my love that followed, sought him out,
On strange, mysterious, dim and awful paths,
And dwelled beside him, never seen nor heard,
Yet ever by some swift, unerring sense
Made known to him.

And thus there came at last
The happy day wherein I too was called,
When from me too there dropped away forever
The poor, worn raiments of mortality.
— On a green bank, beside a gentle stream,
I first awoke again from that brief sleep
They call eternal there below, — awoke
To find a loved, lost, unforgotten form
Kneeling beside me, bending over me, —
To meet an eye radiant with infinite love, —
His form, his face, his eye! — His, his, oh God,
Saved, purified, redeemed, made whole and new
By Thy deep miracle of Grace, surpassing,

Incomprehensible! — Oh Friend, Sweet Soul,
What need to say aught more, or strive to paint
The tearful storm of blinding ecstasy,
Wherewith we rushed into each other's arms, —
Speechless, yet knowing all! —

                        My tale is told,
And those dark memories fade and flee behind me,
Never, mayhap, to be called up again!
— Look thou, the golden flush of evening deepens
O'er hill and vale and stream, and see, ah see,
There from the lengthening shadows of the wood,
Come our dear Loves! — Mine with the stately step,
And royal mien, and selfsame sunny smile,
That won me first! — Oh, I beseech thee, Friend,
Call me not foolish, nor yet smile in turn,
But to this hour I cannot always look
Without glad tears on that most noble form,
That now indeed but visibly shows forth
A soul divine as God has ever made! —
— Ah, they perceive us now, and beckon to us,
Hastening their steps! — Oh come, Sweet Soul, arise,
And let us go to meet them! — Love, my Love!

A MAIDEN'S QUESTION.

O STRANGE love! if this be loving such as
    bards have sung for aye,
Since the world their songs have gladdened,
    sprang from darkness into day!

— Naught in all that world more grateful music
    to my thirsting ear
Than his name and fame and praises loudly
    echoed far and near;

Naught in all the world more joyful tiding to
    my waiting soul
Than to know him nigh who wanders like a
    star from pole to pole.

— Yet when satisfied my yearning, face to face
    with him I stand,
See his sunny smile of welcome, feel the pres-
    sure of his hand, —

Then my steady eye unfaltering his clear glance can rise to meet,
No swift flutter stirs my pulses, my still heart no quickened beat.

No fine sense of heightened being, no deep thrill of ecstasy,
No unutterable rapture, with his nearness comes to me.

Only peace, — a calm assurance, whence or how I cannot tell,
Through his power of noble manhood all things must be passing well.

All the currents flow harmonious in the world I half forget,
Grown so brave I go unflinching even from him without regret.

Yet when I have turned and left him, and his form is lost to sight, —
Oh, how fade from all about me, brightness, color, life, and light!

As when dies a strain of music on a sad, gray
    evening shore,
Heaven and earth grow blank and dreary with
    his presence seen no more;

Till from out the dimness slowly gathering shape
    and living hue,
His dear image, clear as morning, rises on my
    inward view.

Steals from night the sleep I gladly offer up as
    I retrace
Every look and tone,—each fleeting light or
    shadow on his face;

Fills the day to overflowing with unspeakable
    content,
Lets the hours seem rich that idly dreaming but
    of him were spent;

Gives all life a patient courage no dark power
    shall now destroy,
For the thought of him has made me strong in
    everlasting joy.

So the year rolls round fulfilling my fond hope,
    — we meet once more,
And the peace, the sadness, gladness, steal upon
    me as before.

O dear bards who sing of loving, — or your-
    selves, great gods above, —
Solve unto my soul this riddle, — help me, —
    tell me, — *is this love?*

SURRENDER.

Away, heart-breaking struggle, vain control!
Wholly, without reserve, resistlessly,
I yield for all eternity my soul,
Oh deathless current of my love, to thee!
Whose throbbing waves about me swell and roll
Like the dark waters of a fretful sea,
Never, 'neath sun's glow, nor the stars' cold light,
Sleeping or resting, day or dawn or night!

Yet oh, dear miracle! — what once most sore
And deadly conflict made me, such fierce fray,
That broken, breathless, bleeding at each pore,
I through its sullen fury scarce my way
Clove to some shelter on the barren shore, —
Now bears me in a gently rocking sway,
And laps me with soft ripples, that my breast
Play round about, with grateful sense of rest.

Oh blest surrender! Passing sweet release
From aching toil, but thou abandonment
Couldst bring the storm-tossed soul, to whom surcease
Of pain is joy!— Whereto thy course is bent,
I care not!— Bear me to despair or peace,
Life, death, or infinite bliss, I am content
To drift forever thus, wide heaven above,
On thy deep current, oh my deathless love!

YEARNING.

I LAID my ear close to the cold, bare ground,
Where grow the sturdy oak and branching vine,
Listening if at their roots might not be found
A feeble stir, though in the air the fine
Sharp breath of winter lingered still. And ay,
Methought that deep, deep down, faint, far away
Even as the warble of a bird, so high
Lost in the stainless blue of dewy day
That eye may never follow it, I caught
A fluttering throb of new, sweet life set free
And soon to quicken swelling buds. — Oh thought
Of rapture and divinest ecstasy,
Oh blest, unfailing promise, that must bring
The light and lays and fragrant blossoming,
All nameless joys of golden, white-starred Spring!

Oh could I thus upon thy great, warm heart,
Rich in the noblest pith of manhood's flower,
Where strength and tenderness have equal part,

Lay down my yearning head for one brief hour!
And catch each faintest sound that upward stole
With eager ear, and find if there below,
In the most secret pulses of thy soul,
Where the deep founts of life and being flow,
There stirs, mayhap, faint, dim, and far away
Even as the distant Spring's sweet ecstasy,
'Mid the chill breath of some dark winter-day,
A quickening thrill of answering love for me!
— Oh bliss unspeakable, undreamed, untold!
I have no answer but the gushing tear,
To what in one sweet whisper would unfold
The blossomed wealth of all the rolling year,
Oh thou who by a breath transfiguring
All heaven and earth, my thirsting soul couldst bring,
The deathless joys of everlasting Spring!

A FLOWER OF HOPE.

Sitting that day before the ruddy fire,
He read what to my eager soul was sweet
As honey to the lips, and melody
To the charmed ear, — praise of his noble art
And high achievements. For a little time
The deep, rich cadences rolled smooth and strong,
Like a broad river gentle in its power;
But suddenly the even, steadfast voice
Faltered and fell and ceased, and looking up,
I in mute, startled wonderment beheld
The clear eyes dim with overbrimming tears!

Oh friend, dear friend, forgive the yearning soul,
That reaches out towards thine
With every fibre thrilling and aglow,
And yet could not divine

What in that sad, sweet hour stirred secretly,
The well-springs of thy heart! —

Was it the coming hour when we must speak
A brief farewell and part?

Or the dim consciousness that thou and I
Could never meet again
Giving the same frank clasp of hands wherewith
We met and parted then? —

Never again, while the mute lips of both
Must hold in silence sealed,
Untold, unbreathed, all that the braver eye
Had mayhap half revealed? —

Ah, who shall guess? — I only know that from
Those dear, dark tears of thine
Sprang a pale, tender, trembling flower of hope,
So frail and over-fine,

And yet so fragrant, that though one rude blast
Smote it with sudden death,
I dare not let the intoxicated sense
Drink in its full, sweet breath;

I dare not tend, nor yet can let it fade
In rain or drought or sun,

Lest as it drooped and died, my own poor soul
Were utterly undone!

For through thy tears, oh friend, were in that soul
The secret streams set free
Of all that deepest life which sets towards thine
Through all eternity!

INSUFFICIENCY.

Like a harp where the Great Master set rich chords both deep and strong,
That give forth heroic measures, kingly chant and solemn song, —

But some finer strings are missing, never set, or it may be
Snapped in early days and tender, by some tempest ruthlessly, —

Is thy soul, oh my Beloved! ever rendering back to mine,
But a strange, harsh tune I know not, from those chords more strong than fine.

Yet beloved still! — ay better, than if all were well with thee,
Fonder, truer, oh my darling, for the need thou hast of me!

For thou need'st me, thirstest for me, oh my harp with missing strings,
As we thirst for cooling waters from Life's Everlasting Springs!

Those deep chords thrill with a yearning, haply to themselves unknown,
To respond in rarest music, to the sweetness of my own.

Oh, and sometime when dim earth-life fades from out our gladdened view,
The great Master Hand shall gently fashion thee, dear harp, anew!

To my faithful hand committing that fair, perfect instrument,
Till our strings together chiming, in one rapturous song are blent,

And thus blending, oh Beloved, make such heavenly harmony,
Chanting angel-choirs shall, pausing, joyful list to thee and me!

SONNETS.

I.

I CANNOT lose thee! Though we dwelled apart
Leagues upon leagues of endless sea and shore,
Though through long years no message came that bore
Of thee glad tidings, telling where thou art, —
Still thy dumb absence could not bring a smart
To my brave soul, for from its inmost core
Springs the fine band that knits us evermore.
A hopeful patience, foreign to the heart
Wont to rush forward all too eagerly,
Goes with me day and night, a faith sublime
As deep as life, more strong than death or time,
Till what divides us now, the sky and sea
  Themselves, seem to repeat the blest refrain, —
So sure as God lives, we shall meet again!

II.

I cannot lose thee! Though between thy heart
And mine a legion of black phantoms lay,
Like a grim host of foes in war's array, —
In vain the bristling lance or swift-winged dart,
To strike my dauntless soul a bleeding smart.
No earthly power my eagerness could stay
From cutting through ten thousand foes a way
That should unerring lead me where thou art,
Armed by the faith sublime that thou and I
Are knit by bands that time and death defy,
Invincible, as to my ear grows plain
What must ere long roll forth a loud refrain,
    Swelling to heaven from joyous sea and shore, —
    So sure as God lives, we shall part no more!

THE FACE OF GOD.

TO —— ——.

Lo! from the deep of the fair, cloudless sky,
Where thy proud sun of fame
In undimmed noonday splendor blazed on high,
Close to the stars, — there came

A swift-winged dart that pierced thy panoply,
And bade thee kiss the ground,
And brought a cloud whose shadow suddenly
Quenched all the brightness round.

Till rising on one knee with blinded sight,
Thou an imploring hand
Throw'st out, as if to stay the smarting night
Thou canst not understand.

And yet rejoice, my stricken King, as I
With all my soul rejoice,

For in that shadow draws a Presence nigh
And sounds an awful Voice,

That we may not perceive, Beloved One,
When fair are sky and sod,
When all too dazzling shines the noonday sun
That hides the Face of God!

A WELL OF SORROW.

Ah, the memory of thy living and thy dying, dear my friend,
Of thy manhood warped and broken, of the bitter, hopeless end, —

Is like some black well, one instant flashing in the sun's glad light
'Neath a shower of golden sparkles, soon gone out in gloomier night!

Like a well of sorrow, quenchless, never yet run low or dry,
Where our thoughts like doves, though wheeling with white wings against the sky

Fair with blue and warm with sunshine, still drawn hither evermore,
Come to drink of grief like water, from that deep, exhaustless store.

Ay, so deep and dark and bitter, one small drop
    shall have the power,
Even when tides of life run highest, in some
    maddest, merriest hour,

Swift as death to wilt the roses twined about the
    goblet's brim,
Hush the jest, the song, the laughter, make the
    lustrous eye grow dim,

Send the chill of disenchantment to the sudden
    sobered heart,
Fill it with a secret hunger, but to sit and weep
    apart,

Weep while life endures and memory, tears wrung
    from our souls like blood.
And yet, lo! — thus gazing downward far into
    that troubled flood,

We behold with joyful wonder, that where shad-
    ows thickest press,
There our love and grief and yearning, and the
    infinite tenderness

Of the God of passing Mercy, on that fount's
 black bosom shine,
Clearly mirrored, never shaken, radiant like sweet
 stars divine!

THROUGH THE MIDNIGHT SKY.

Through the faint-gleaming midnight sky,
Deep beyond deep above,
My yearning soul soars up on high,
To seek thy soul, O Love!

Thy soul to joy or sorrow bound,
Which dwells I know not where,
Only that it is folded round
By God's eternal care.

And that this hour He sets thee free,
Even from the furthest star
Through boundless space to come to me
Who wait thee, from afar.

And by the sudden touch of fire
That on my heart is laid,
Till with the strength of its desire
It trembles, half afraid,—

I know while swiftly draw more nigh,
The gleaming deeps above,
Our souls beneath the silent sky
Have met and kissed, O Love!

GOD'S PEACE.

Dead! A great hope is dead
From whose fair eyes o'er all the years to come,
A starry light was shed;—
The smile forever fled,
The soft voice hushed, the lips grown white and dumb,
Cold the warm hands that wove bright, fragrant flowers,
Even through the thorns of day's most weary hours!

Oh heart, how desolate!
Where the tear-blinded, helpless eye may turn,
Earth, sea and sky, so late
In all the royal state
Of Springtime's full-flushed splendors wont to burn,
Sunk to gray ashes, now that beauteous head,
Strewed with dim dust, lies in its narrow bed!

But, oh sweet marvel! — low
About the grave, 'mid blighting **frost and rime**
Still brave with purple **glow,**
Courage and patience **grow;**
And, green through Winter and through **Summer time,**
Faith high, immortal **stands,**
With upward pointing hands,
A noble tree, through whose broad-spreading crown
God's Peace, like golden sunshine, filters down.

HYMN.

I THINK Thou lovest me, Lord,
   For thy dear mercy all my pains hath cured, —
Nay, granted me exceeding great reward
   For the sharp ills endured.

I think it by the joy
   That fills my soul on this dark winter day, —
The golden peace no grief shall now destroy,
   No tempest blow away.

The thorns that pricked me sore
   Turned in my hands to blossoms white and sweet,
The flinty stones my pathway led me o'er,
   Soft turf beneath my feet.

The cup of gall has grown —
   Oh, passing miracle! — to honeyed wine,

And on my trembling lips the bitter moan,
   Into a song divine.

I know Thou lovest me, Lord, —
   Yea, though these eyes wept tears of blood
      awhile, —
For I can look upon the cruel sword
   That smote my heart, and smile.

INTO THY HANDS.

Into Thy Hands, my Father, I commit
   All, all my spirit's care,
   The sorest burden this dim life can bear,
The sweetest hope wherewith its paths are lit!
Into Thy Hands, that hold so closely knit
   What our blind, aching heart
   Calls joy or grief, — we know them not apart!
Into the Hands whence leap
   The hurling tempest, and the gentle breath
Kissing the babe to sleep,
   The flaming bolt that smites with instant death
The giant oak, and the refreshing shower
Whose balmy drops make glad the tender flower.

What though, even as lent jewels passing bright,
   That crowned me happy king
   For one sweet revel of one night in spring,
I must surrender in the morning light,

That cold and gray breaks on my tearful sight,
  Youth, hope, and joy, and love,
  And — oh, all other gems, all price, above! —
The deathless certainty
  Of the deep life beyond this pallid sun,
That golden shore and sea
  Which to my youthful feet seemed wellnigh
      won,
So fair, so close, so clear, methought I heard
The trees' soft whisper and faint song of bird.

What though this fair dream, too, fled long ago
  And on my straining eyes
  There break no more visions of mellow skies
'Neath which dear friends, called dead, move on
      in low
Sweet converse, through wide, happy fields aglow
  With heavenly flower and star, —
  What though, like some poor pilgrim who from
      far
Sees, through a slender rift
  In the dark rocks that hem his toilsome way,
The clouds an instant lift
  From countries bathed in everlasting day,
I stand and stretch my yearning arms in vain
Toward the blest light, too swiftly lost again?

Into Thy Hands, my Father, I commit
    This dearest, last hope too,
    Old as the world, and yet forever new, —
The hope wherewith our dimmest paths are lit,
With life itself indissolubly knit!
    That too is well, I know,
    In Thy eternal keeping. Ah! and so
Let my poor soul dismiss
    Each fear and doubt, hush every anxious cry,
Forget all thought save this,
    Some time, — oh, dream of joy that cannot die! —
In those beloved Hands, a priceless store,
All our lost jewels shall be found once more!

SONNET.

APOLLO, — Jupiter, — Jehovah, — God!
What matter by what name we call on Thee,
Incomprehensible Divinity,
Unfathomed by us children of the clod
Now, as when man the first fair meadows trod,
Fresh from Thy hand! Deeper than sea on sea,
Far off as heaven, vast as eternity,
Yet present in the grasses of the sod, —
So we but worship something more sublime
Than our poor selves, give the too haughty soul
To something that outreaches earth and time,
And what sharp ills our fleeting lives control,
Endure in patience 'neath thy thorny rod,
Apollo, — Jupiter, — Jehovah, — God!

THE HERB FORGETFULNESS.

"Wo wächst das Kraut Vergessenheit?"

"Where grows the herb Forgetfulness,
    O Mother, dost thou know?
On sun-scorched soil no foot may press,
    Or 'mid eternal snow?

"In some still nook the tempests shun,
    Or on the wind-swept plain?
Lit by what pallid midnight sun,
    Fed by what dew or rain,

"Springs the white flower from whose deep heart
    A wondrous draught distilled,
Has power to soothe each throbbing smart,
    Each yearning unfulfilled;

"All tears to dry, all wounds make whole,
    All founts of sorrow seal;
The bitterest anguish of the soul,
    Love's hopeless pangs to heal?

"O'er all the world I'd wander round,
   Through day and night as well,
To learn where that sweet balm be found.
   O Mother, canst thou tell?"

"Ay, child. The path is steep and slow,
   Yet brave and patient feet
Will carry thee where thou may'st know
   That blossom bitter-sweet.

"The herb that brings forgetfulness,
   And makes all wounds grow whole,
And sends God's Peace to soothe and bless
   The hopeless travailing soul,

"And has immortal power to still
   The fiercest wind and tide,
Springs at the foot of that dark Hill
   Where Christ was crucified."

THY WILL BE DONE.

Blow on, fierce tempest, blow!
Pour down thy drenching rain,
Flash thy red lightning's glow
O'er trembling land and main, —
I, but an humble lily of the field,
Resistless to thy swinging furies yield,
Let without pause or stay
All bonds and fetters burst,
Wild winds and torrents sway,
Wreak on my head their worst!

What though they snap and drown
Blossom and branch and root,
Wither and blast far down
Fair bud and tender shoot, —
From my crushed, broken heart may still rise up,
Like incense from a shivered golden cup,
A last faint breath to Heaven.
Left without star or sun, —
He took what He had given,
Thy will, my God, be done!

MY FATHER'S CHILD.

Though ye do no wonderful deeds and accomplish no great sacrifices, it shall be sufficient unto you, to have worshipped the Lord with your whole heart and strength.

About her head or floating feet
   No halo's starry gleam,
Still dark and swift uprising, like
   A bubble in a stream, —

A soul from whose rejoicing heart
   The bonds of earth were riven,
Sped upward through the silent night
   To the closed Gates of Heaven.

And waiting heard a voice — "Who comes
   To claim Eternity?
Hero or saint that bled and died
   Mankind to save and free?"

She bent her head. The voice once more —
   "Didst thou then toil and live

For home and children — to thy Love
    Last breath and heart's-blood give?"

Her head sank lower still, she clasped
    Her hands upon her breast —
"Oh, no!" she whispered, "my dim life
    Has never been so blest!

"I trod a lonely, barren path,
    And neither great nor good,
Gained not a hero's palm, nor won
    The crown of motherhood!

"Oh, I was naught!" Yet suddenly
    The white lips faintly smiled —
"Save, oh, methinks I was mayhap
    My Heavenly Father's Child!"

A flash of light, a cry of joy,
    And with uplifted eyes
The soul through gates rolled open wide,
    Passed into Paradise.

AFTER YEARS.

"For what is a man profited if he shall gain the whole world and yet lose his own soul?" — ST. MATTHEW.

BE thine, thy wife? Forever bound to thee
In that most awful, closest bond, where blend
Soul, body, heart, and spirit, — called to be
One flesh, one life? Impossible! Oh, friend,
Forgive me, but I cannot, must not now! —
Not now accept what once with ecstasy
Unspeakable had thrilled me, made the brow
Whereon thy touch left some sweet majesty
Prouder than any queen's!
                   And dost thou say
I love thee not, and never loved thee? — Nay,
God knows 't is not well said, thou dost me wrong! —
Knows how I lavishly poured at thy feet
The richest blood wherewith my heart was strong
Because I called it thine! With what complete,

AFTER YEARS.

Undoubting, patient, hopeful constancy
I clung to thee, how fondly and how long,
Until that fondness seemed to sap and drain
All life itself within me, and I fain
Had cried for truce and mercy. They have come,
The peace and rest I craved! It is too late,
All voices pleading for thee once are dumb,
Voices whose sweetest music scarce could sate
The heart so deeply thirsting. The fair rose
That only once in full-flushed glory blows,
Has blown and withered, blasted past restore,—
The God who smites and heals,—or call it fate,
Dark destiny that vainly we deplore,—
Has parted us forever!

      And wherefore
Too late, thou ask'st? (Nay, but I will not
  pause,
I must push on even to the harshest end,
And thou, I think, wilt pardon me!) Because
I see too clearly now! And oh, my friend,
God, God knows, too, at what uncounted cost
Of buried hopes, and faith forever lost,
That dear-bought clearness came! What floods
  of tears
Washed these poor eyes, too long and fondly
  blind,

Ere they had such sharp vision, but to find
The light of truth, slow-breaking after years,
Even then smote with intolerable sting
The aching sight. God is my judge for aye, —
(I cannot even yet, remembering,
Speak calmly of it all! Pardon, I pray,
The husky voice, and this quick, broken breath!)
How I hung back and wavered ere I took,
With parched and fevered lips, and hands that
    shook, —
Took, broke and tasted, finding that it burned
More fiercely bitter than the pang of death,
That fruit with ashes filled, which yet I learned
To eat at last even as my daily bread,
The fruit of the conviction too long spurned,
That we, — that thou and I, could never wed,
Because (God! had I never lived to see!)
My heart has finer fibres than thy own!
(The word is uttered now that falls on me,
And oh, I sadly fear, on me alone,
Like a sharp, smarting blow!) — So much more
    fine,
That thy poor heart has frayed and wounded
    mine
A thousand times, and never guessed nor known
How often bruised and bleeding mine forgave, —

So much more fine (oh let me still be brave!)
I may speak this which makes my spirit groan,
And never touch thee to the quick!

                                      Most true,
Christ did not thus! He never walked apart
From those who had most need of him, and drew
His white robes close about his life-warm heart,
Crying, "Nay, friend, I am too good for thee!"
But Christ was Christ, and his humanity
Wrought of such subtlest essence past compare,
That through it knit to God insolubly,
Men not unjustly call him the divine.
And Christ was never wed, — not thus would share
And mingle in the lot of those he gave
His priceless blood, but not his soul, to save!
I am but made of common clay, and mine
Is but a woman's heart, though now set free,
How should I venture that which even he
Dared not attempt!

                       And hast thou lost me then?
No, as I live, friend, no! — Oh thou wast planned
Nobler than one in twenty thousand men! —
Thou hast not lost me, — pray thee take my hand,

(Ah, thank thee for that strong warm clasp of
    thine !) —
Most nobly planned, but God's supreme design
Was sadly blurred and twisted, wrenched away
From His grand primal purpose ; — how and why
Let us not question ! — Yet for all and all
Thou canst not lose what must beyond recall
Through chance and change and storms be thine
    for aye,
The fond and faithful love that cannot die !
For I do love thee still, though may not give
What thou would'st ask in answer to thine own,
Whose barren blossoms now, too late, have
    blown,
Thy love, that once I thought I could not live
Unless I won ! — I love thee still, O friend,
But dare not yield thee that which God to me
Granted a sacred trust, eternally
Held dear as heaven itself, — which in the end
I must surrender back to his control
Flawless and stainless, — my immortal soul !

HOPE.

Hope fluttered for an instant at my door,
Like some blithe bird from sunny Southern shore,

For one brief moment perched upon my sill,
With many a warble and soft, joyous trill;

But yet, ere I could ope, and bid him stay,
He spread his shining wings and soared away

Into the golden skies far out of sight,
Where eye may follow not his boundless flight.

CUPID.

"What stranger comes so late with timid tapping,
 To knock upon my door?
How, is it love? Surely I had not fancied
 To ever see him more!

"Nay, but my pretty, rosy, smiling cherub,
 Who now dost slyly stand,
To thy arch lips pressing one chubby finger,
 The other dimpled hand

"Holding thy cunning bow, while o'er thy shoulder
 The painted quiver peeps,
Whose wicked darts many a poor heart shall startle
 That now securely sleeps.

"From dancing curls and eyes with laughter brimming
 Down to the twinkling feet,

The sunlight bathing thee in golden glory, —
  I pray thee hence, my sweet!

"Believe me, here can be for thee no dwelling;
  I conjure thee, away!
The chambers of my house are dark and silent,
  'T is many a long, chill day

"Since they were thrown wide open with glad welcome
  To such a guest as thee!"
— So cried the maid. But he nor heard nor heeded,
  But more impatiently

Knocked ever loud and louder, frowned and pouted,
  And, full of wrath at last,
Burst through the bolts and bars that, I much fear me,
  Were none too well made fast!

And now it seemed, grown to a very giant,
  Strode through both court and hall,
With steps that made the silent chambers echo,
  And tremble every wall.

And now seized a swift torch and suddenly
  Kindled the timbers dry
With a great flame that crackling, roaring, blazing,
  Flared upward to the sky.

Then sped away ere he could singe his winglets,
  And turning back to see
What mischief he had wrought, laughed long and loudly,
  Clapping his hands with glee.

YOUNG LOVE.

O what a loss is here, past all repair,
   Though thousand years of sunshine were mine own,
Ne'er to have known young love when life was fair,
   In the first flush of morn that long has flown!

What though his hands heaped high with gems, he yet
   Should come to me in fullness of his powers,—
Could all their lustre make my soul forget
   The dewy freshness of those early flowers?

The fragrance fine that from his garment streams,
   The passing sweetness in those blossoms found?—
His noble brow whereon a fillet gleams,
   The youthful god with simple garlands crowned?—

O never, never! Thirst for aye unstilled
   Through all eternity!— For e'en the wide
Rich heavens, were all their promises fulfilled,
   Could never grant the boon that earth denied!

HIS WILL, NOT MINE.

"The love of all
Is but a small thing to the love of one!"
MRS. BROWNING.

O FOND glad dream of brighter, bygone days,
   Too often dreamed of yore, —
That sometime mayhap all these idle lays
   Were hushed, and heard no more!

Sometime this fever of unrest might cease,
   That goads my weary soul
Forever on without or pause or peace,
   To an immortal goal.

That sometime merged in thine, O Love, and lost
   As brooks with streams are blent,
Might find at last my spirit, tempest-tossed,
   Unspeakable content!

That dwelling close to thy immortal heart,
   Should surely prove to be —

Grown of its deeper life a slender part —
   Greatness enough for me.

Yet God's dear mercy did not thus ordain,
   But bid the poor, frail vine,
That stretched its yearning tendrils out in vain
   Round the strong stem to twine,

Itself to harden to a tree, and bide
   All the fierce storms He sent, —
The brooklet with the noble river's tide
   Forevermore unblent,

Its waters widening, deepening as they passed,
   Itself a stream to flow, —
Bid that my being should itself at last
   To feeble greatness grow.

And so these lays sound on till with their strain
   A thousand homes are filled,
While I, a wandering bird, have sought in vain
   My own bright nest to build.

How may from thirst the parching lips be saved,
   But slowly gathering up,
In scanty drops, the draught of life they craved
   In one o'erbrimming cup!

The wide world's praises, O what bitter bliss,
  To the great love of one, —
And oh, God knows, God knows that in all this,
  His will, not mine, was done!

SHIPWRECKED.

I too have hoped and dared! — My heart throbbed
    high
When once at dewy morn I took my place
Among the youths who to the rose-flushed sky
Smiling above, lifted such radiant face
It seemed Jove's darkest thunders to defy. —
But all have far outstripped me in the race,
Left me with aching feet and weary soul,
To reach as best I might the fading goal.

I too have toiled and striven! — With patient
    hand
Guided the laboring plow, that drew its slow,
Deep furrows in the earth, tilled all my land,
Scattered good seed, watered and watched it
    grow, —
The barns of hundred others bursting stand
With their rich harvests' golden overflow,
While I scarce glean toil's scant and mournful
    meed,
The few poor grains sufficient for my need!

I too have loved and sung!— A lay may be,
As sweet and strong, as tender, deep, and fair
As aught the world to-day hears eagerly, —
Yet the light songs of others everywhere,
Are joyful echoed over land and sea,
While mine die vainly on the empty air,
I, a lone nightingale in some dark glade,
Suffer and sing and perish in the shade!

Fame, fortune, love, and love's dear joys, all, all
A barren hope, a shivered dream, no more!
Dead as the heavy leaves that withered fall
When from gray skies the rains of autumn pour,
Whose poor, spent life no spring-tide shall recall, —
Shipwrecked the bark that bravely left the shore,
All lost at sea, far from the vanished goal,
Save only God, and my immortal soul!

LOVE HAS DECEIVED ME.

Love has deceived me! — With a strange, sweet
    smile,
  He took from out my yielding hand the oar
Wherewith I thought to guide for many a mile
  My bark through sunlit waters close to
    shore.
"Come, I will speed thee to the Blessed Isle!"
  He said, and smiled again, but spoke no
    more, —
And suddenly I found me far from land,
Aground upon a bank of barren sand!

And yet he came again, and charmed from me
  The sword wherewith through rugged rocks I
    thought
To carve a path to some high destiny,
  The deathless goal that long my soul had sought.
"Come," said he gently, "come, and thou shalt
    see
  Beside my joys all others sink to naught!"

And, blindly following, suddenly I stood
Forsaken in a dark, entangled wood!

Then he stole on me like a thief at night,
   And seized the shuttle from my clinging hold,
Wherewith I wove a cloth perchance not bright,
   Yet strong and fine. "I'll make a woof with gold
And purple shot," he said, and in my sight
   Charmed forth what seemed rich fabrics, fold on fold,
Till I perceived he spun with cunning care
A glittering nothing of the empty air.

Love has undone me! Oh, how should I meet
   Tempests and foes with pride and strength laid low
And arms all shivered? And, oh, worst defeat,
   Sum of all ills the stricken heart may know,
The secret sense that naught is half so sweet
   As his soft voice who is my deadliest foe,
Naught half so beauteous 'neath the sun to see
As his fair eyes, all traitors though they be!

MARIANA.

"' He cometh not!' she said."

HE never came whose step and loving call
    I waited long to hear,
But thou hast come, last Messenger of all,
    A friend wellnigh as dear!

Peace if not joy!—yet peace itself were gain,
    That must supremely bless
The soul sore travailed, that in vain, in vain
    Hungered for happiness!

Draw closer, oh thou voiceless Guest and pale,
    Whose drooping torch burns low:
Thy face is hid, but through the sombre veil
    Thine eyes' dark light I know!

Nay, closer still!—I yearn on brow and heart
    Thy cool, strong hand to feel;

Fevered with wounds, and throbbing with a
    smart
  Thy touch alone can heal.

I go with joy! Lead me to him at last, —
  How dim the path and lone —
Him, whose far footsteps, echoing through the
    past,
  Have never met mine own.

THE SILENT HOUSE.

It all was over, and the house was still. —
The hearse had rolled away, the friends were
        gone,
Their vacant seats looked blank and desolate. —
— The muffled mirror hung against the wall,
The spot was empty where the bier had stood
Whereon he lay with mute and smiling lips. —
— And naught remained of him who once had
        been
The light of soul, the staff of life to me,
Naught but the cross, that had been left behind,
Of odorless, white flowers, — so dead, so dead. —
And nothing now remained but I alone,
Alone to live the long, long, joyless days. —
And so with weary feet I climbed the stair,
Up to the room where he was wont to sit.
— The silent books upon their long-rowed shelves,
The fair, white marbles in their quiet niche,
Beside his pen, a bunch of withered flowers,

The ivy twining round the window frame,
The noiseless floor where oft his feet had trod,
The motes of dust that danced within the light, —
All was so dead, so dead ; — and nothing stirred
Save at the pane an idly buzzing fly,
And in his cage the blithe canary-bird,
That hopped and pecked, and wondering looked at me.
— The golden flecks of sunset on the wall
Moved high and higher till they touched his cage
With purple light, — the little bird burst forth
In loud, rejoicing song, and I in tears. —

The morning sun was in the room, — I woke, —
I knew it was a dream, — I knew my life,
Was heavier than the burden of my dream, —
— I had not won, I had not loved nor lost. —

SONG.

Oh, does my love love thee, great Queen,
    Upon thy lofty throne,
Where shine, more bright than sunset clouds,
    Red gold and ruby stone?
Did he fold thee in his strong arms
    Close to his brave, warm heart,
And whisper words more sweet than life? —
    Ah God, — how poor thou art!

Me, me he chose, the lowly one,
    From all the glittering train
That caught the sunshine of his smile,
    But sought his soul in vain!
Oh, though thy empire were the world,
    All earth and sea and sky,
Poor Queen, my heart would bleed for thee,
    So rich, — ah God, am I!

LOVE ME.

Love me as thou may'st love the silvery light
Of some far, shimmering moonbeam faint and
    small,
That glides across thy foot on summer night, —
— O love, but do not love me not at all ! —

Love me as thou didst love, a little child,
The grasses on the meadow high and tall,
Or blossoms in the forest, sweet and wild, —
O love, but do not love me not at all ! —

Love me as some faint music far away,
That pleasantly upon thy ear may fall,
At stilly eve of some long, weary day, —
— O love, but do not love me not at all ! —

Love me as the swift shadow of the feet
Of her who should have been thy all in all,
As she some other loved one flew to meet, —
— O love, but do not love me not at all ! —

SORROW.

Sorrow, my brave companion true and tried,
  My earliest, latest, and most constant friend,
My childhood's playmate, and my youth's stern
    guide,
  Who wilt not part till day is at an end —
Do I again so close to me behold
Thy rugged brow, not young yet never old?

Joy, love, and hope were left behind us long,
  Too frail, they drooped upon the sun-scorched
    way,
Or perished in the storm; but thou art strong:
  Tempest, nor cloud, nor thirst, nor heat of day
Wearies thy patience; morn and eventide,
Steadfast and faithful, found thee at my side.

If for an hour sometimes I missed thy face,
  And hastening forward climbed a sunlit height,

Where my glad soul enraptured would embrace
   The fair, sweet world, grown wide with new
      delight,
Thy touch upon my heart quenched suddenly
The golden splendors of the earth and sea.

And yet I thank thee, messenger of God!
   For thou shalt ease, when day is at an end,
That last dim path that must by all be trod,
   Blind, mute, alone, without a single friend, —
Where e'en thy feet must pause, thy service done,
   Oh my brave comrade, thou most faithful one!
Close to the Gates that shut from thy grave eyes
The Land beyond with its unclouded skies!

MEASURE FOR MEASURE.

"O, YES!" the throng of eager listeners cried,
And gathered close the gray, old Bard beside.

"Come tell us some good tale!" "A tale," said he,
And sadly smiled. "A tale you ask of me!

"But, friends, I fear me I have none to tell
That when you hear shall please you over-well.

"But as you will! A noble Prince one day
Awoke in a strange country, far away

"From his dear native land: what stern decree
To these rude shores exiled him suddenly

"He knew not, nor on what fair star had been
That first bright home his happy eyes had seen;

"But dimly, like a half-remembered dream,
Its tufted palms and golden waters' gleam

"Came back upon his yearning soul, that here
Found earth and sea and sky but chill and drear.

"And all that now recalled to him the great
Forgotten splendors of his royal state,

"Was a wide flask of rarest, precious wine,
Clear as the sun, deep as the ruby's shine,

"And a gemmed cup, fashioned with curious art.—
Yet strong in vigorous youth and brave of heart,

"Bearing his sole possessions in his hand,
He wandered through the world, o'er sea and land,

"Unknown of all, simple in garb and glance
Like those he walked among, save that perchance

"A silent majesty upon his brow,
That wore the shadow of a crown e'en now,

"Marked him the scion of a kingly race.
And where in town or wood or field, what place

"He came on men, he lavishly held up
And filled with his gold wine the o'er-brimming
    cup,

"And pledged them all and bid them joyfully
'Bring out your best, e'en as I give to ye!'

"They drank to him in turn, swift to obey
The summons, kind enough in their sad way,

"But in the Prince's heart e'er lived the thought,
'Great God, how poor they are!' seeing they
    brought

"But shallow goblets made of brittle glass,
Or cups of common metal, tin and brass;

"And when he tasted of their proffered draught,
He found 'twas pale, flat water that he quaffed,

"While they, his wine scarce touched with lips,
    cut wry
Strange faces, and would shake their heads, and
    hie

"To hand it back to him, or, turning round,
Empty it slyly out upon the ground.

"He wandered thus for many a day and year,
Not joyful as at first, nor full of cheer,

"Yet ever by undying hope led on,
Through gathering twilight and gray, starless dawn;

"But evermore deceived by all the throng
That crossed his path; and though his life was long,

"Even when his hair turned white, his eye grew dim,
Measure for measure none had given to him!"

"Well, and what then? The end?" his hearers said,
As now the old bard paused and bent his head.

Another smile, and sadder than before,
Passed o'er his lips: "Good friends, I know no more!

"What was the Prince's end I cannot say,
Save that perchance, late on a wintry day,

"His empty flask beside him, he was found
Dead by the roadside on the barren ground."

"Oh, but who was he, pray?" they asked again.
"Give us his name! And who those other men?"

But now his eye lit up with sudden scorn
As he cried out, "See here the kingly born!

"And look around upon yourselves to find
Those villagers of shallow heart and mind!"

And rising, turned his back on them, while they
Gazed after him in open-mouthed dismay.

THE STROLLING PLAYER.

"The man, becoming troubled in his mind, traveled East and West through the country for some time, in the vain hope of obtaining an engagement, and one morning was found dead in his bed." — *Chronicles of the Stage.*

"Well, I have come!" he cried and gazed
  Upon the empty air;
"You wished me here to show my art, —
  I am a strolling player!

"I can draw tears and laughter both,
  And speak immortal rhymes, —
Who wants me here?" he cried again,
"You've heard me thousand times!"

But empty air alone replied;
  The world, grown dumb and blind,
In pity weeping, turns its head
From the poor, wandering mind.

So passing from closed door to door,
He strikes his weary brow,
And stands bewildered still at last, —
"Strange, — no one wants me now!"

Then suddenly rings a joyful shout, —
"Welcome, dear strolling player!"
And on his troubled eye bursts forth
A scene surpassing fair.

Round him a dome, vast, filled with light,
And rising tier on tier,
Illustrious spirits there convened,
To see his art and hear.

He moves and smiles and would unfold
His noblest, tenderest page, —
And suddenly knows he has been called
To an Immortal Stage!

THE OLD POET'S REST.

SONNET.

Lie fallow for awhile, my brave old brain,
Who long hast served me, and most faithfully,
In sketch and story, song and tragedy,
With toil ofttimes, and bitter pangs and pain,
Yet not so well for all that I could gain
Even from the finest flower that sprang from thee,
Honey to spread my loaf! — Now happily
Lie fallow till the dew and wind and rain
Bring thee new strength, and generous life the sun,
And if I live, I'll sometime glean from there
A richer math, please God, than yet was won;
And if I die, still will I not despair,
For shall not all eternity be mine
Wherein to sing a thousand songs divine?

DESIRE.

Would that love's sun were set,
With it the thrill of pain,
Would it were set to rise
Never again!

Never again to fling
Glory o'er land and sea,—
Left me in starless night,
Wretched and free!

TRUST ME NOT, LOVE.

Trust me not, love; I am but fickle, fickle!
Too easily turns my soul's swift-changing hue;
I cannot long be constant, kind or true!
    Tender or proud and cold,
    Fiery and young or old,
    Filled or with hopes or fears,
    Laughter or bitter tears,
My heart is tossed by every passing breeze!

Now, at high noon, I love the crimson rose,
But ah, alas! who knows,
If ere the starry night please me not best
The golden-hearted lily's pallid crest!

This hour I'd joyful lay me down to die
For a dark lustrous eye;
The next may all my heart be stormed and won
By some blue violet hiding from the sun.

To-day I treasure high proud liberty,
To-morrow I may be
The willing vassal of some mighty king,
Holding his glory dear o'er everything.

Ah! now I love thee with consuming fire,
Now, in the dewy morning's early ray,
But who may tell if not ere close of day,
    Before another morn,
    Hot vows be pledged and sworn,
    Eternal faith, my sweet,
    At other, dearer feet?
Trust me not, love; I am but fickle, fickle!

THY HEART IS LIKE THE SUN.

Thy heart is like the sun within the sky,
That makes the whole world bright,
And as thou beam'st on all from there on high,
So I receive thy light. —

Why should I mourn, that like unto the rest
Thou also giv'st to me? —
And yet I weep to think that I am blest,
Like all humanity! —

WHERE HAST THOU GONE, O MY SOUL?

Where hast thou gone, O my soul,
Suddenly vanished and flown
Into dim regions unknown?
Hast thou delved down into the earth's dark
 core,
  Or floated up into the wintry air,
Or plunged into mid-ocean far from shore,
And to return no more?
  Or dost thou follow on in dumb despair
The shadow of his feet through night and morn,
Who has no heed of thee, O soul forlorn?

Where hast thou gone, O my soul,
Secretly stealing away
From this poor prison of clay?
That cold and dumb it stands since thy swift
 flight
  Like a bleak house whose cheery sounds are
   still,

Its windows dark, its hearth no longer bright, —
That what was once delight,
   The voice 'neath which my heart was wont to thrill
E'en as the wind-harp in the breeze's breath,
Moves it no more from this strange living death?

Wherever thou dwellest, O my soul,
In what dim regions unknown,
Thou may'st be wandering alone,
Come back to me from earth, or air, or sea,
O truant soul, without whose quickening fire,
Grief has no sting, and joy no ecstasy,
And phantoms equally
   Are hope content and unfulfilled desire;
Nor death itself were bitter nor life sweet,
E'en in the very shadow of his feet,
Whom thou must follow, follow night and morn,
Though he may heed thee not, O soul forlorn!

SONNET.

Oh sad, sweet, pallid ghost, — if ghost thou art,
Whose voiceless presence still stands at my door,
And casts a shadow o'er the sunlit floor,
And will not be denied, but claims a part
In every joy or pang, — through the loud mart
Or to the silence where my soul would pour
To God its yearnings, following evermore, —
I cannot banish thee! — this shaken heart
Can find no spell wherewith to exorcise
Thy awful power! — the light in other eyes,
Though love smiled there, grows dim and cold;
    I see
Thine own beyond, fixed on me duskily,
And turn to thee, undone by hopeless strife,
Oh sad, sweet ghost, more living than all life!

OH, BAR THY GATES!

"Oh, bar thy gates, my heart, make fast
   Window and port and door,
Lest thy first foes, returned at last,
   Should enter here once more!
The Joy and Grief were wont of old
Their revels in thy courts to hold;
   Through every arch in state
Throng a gay conquering host,
Or like a voiceless ghost
   At hour of midnight late,
Steal to the castle stealthily, and leave
   Its splendors desolate!"

"The gates are fast! The bitter tide
   Of tears that without stay
Once poured its streams here deep and wide,
   Has forced them shut for aye, —
The bolts and bars are gnawed by rust,
The silent courtyard's dim with dust!

Yet round them grasses spring,
And on the ramparts high,
Beneath a cloudless sky,
Some pallid blossoms swing,
And now and then a bird, in its glad course,
Pauses an hour to sing!"

ROME.

Heart of the world! — that like a newborn star
Gleams on the bosom of the world grown old,
And like a deathless flower, unending far
Breathes subtle perfume from a cup of gold, —
Heart of the world, through whose pulsations flow
Beauty's eternal streams through every land, —
Whose quickening throbs first kindled into glow
The fires of freedom, that no cursèd hand
Could wholly quench again, — who wearest for aye
The sign of empire on thy royal brow,
Beyond the power of kings to wrest away, —
What could the craving spirit ask, that thou
From out thy boundless treasures couldst not give,
And how may I dwell far from thee and live!
From youth's first dawn through oh how many a year

Have I not lovèd thee with undying love,
Have I not yearned to lay my eager ear
Where I might catch around me and above
The music of thy deep, majestic beat,
Heart of the world! — How oft in dreams divine
Dreamed I should haste to thee with flying feet,
To fall with joy ineffable at thine,
While bending o'er me with a gracious smile
Thou lovingly shouldst raise and fold me round
With thy strong arms, and shouldst my soul be-
    guile
Into belief, forgetfulness were found
For all its pangs, — for one brief hour to know
The wounds no more, life struck it long ago.

For thou too lovest me! Oh, have I not heard,
In starry nights across the windy sea,
Thy voice that called to me, — the whispered
    word
That softly wooed and promised lavishly
Delights unto the spirit tempest-tossed,
Fair as the magic visions wont to shine
Surpassing bright in childhood's days long lost.
And still I have not come, and still o'er thine
Eternal hills the sunset's purple gold
Flames as it flamed and died for thousand years,

Unseen by me, whose straining eyes behold
Thine image scarce afar through blinding tears;
Far from thy love a fetter bars me still,
Rigid as God's unalterable Will.

How may with aims immortal still be strong
The fainting soul consumed in vain desire,
Heart of the world, for thee! — how with great
 song,
That might leap forth like living, sacred fire,
The parching lips o'erflow, not given by God
For all the trembling prayers they send on high,
To slake their thirst at thy rich, purple flood,
That I would drain to fill and satisfy
These barren veins, wherein, too well I know,
The sap and strength of youth are withering fast,
The fuller tides of being ebbing low.
— Heart of the world! mine own must break at
 last,
If from thy breath new power I may not gain
To bear life's burden and to sing its pain!

SUNDAY.

SONNET.

Oh blessed day! that like a golden isle
Clasped by a cloudless sky and sunny sea,
Liest 'mid the waves of time that endlessly
Fret round about us, — well might thy deep
    smile
Our wearied souls into belief beguile,
Earth were attuned to sweetest harmony,
We drank of passing peace, and should go free
From fate's dark tempest for a little while.
— In thee, named for the proudest stars of all
That shimmering hang on high, life's fevered
    flow
For a brief space glides with such gentle fall
Past the fair blossoms which beside it blow,
That on its restful heart unruffled shine
The widespread heavens, filled with God's breath
    divine!

TO AN UNKNOWN LOVE.

She was a lonely woman. Yet if sometimes gently twitted on her condition, as is the fashion of young folks, she always smiled brightly, and said she knew that *somewhere* in the Universe her Lover was waiting for her.

OH my blessed Love, beloved though unknown, unfound, unseen,
More than all that God has fashioned His sweet heaven and earth between!

Thou of noble form and feature, ample height and girth of limb,
Of that generous mould resembling some rich vessel, to the brim

Filled with golden wine, whose presence, though in secret hid and sealed,
Its fine fragrance, all pervading, to the gladdened sense revealed.

Ay, a soul wherein there blossoms perfect manhood's fairest flower,
Strength to tenderness transmuted, mildness wedded into power.

Of a brow where thoughts immortal set glad youth's unfading spell,
Of a grave, sweet smile, and earnest, quiet eyes, that kindly dwell

On all living things and creatures, men of every clime and zone,
Yet with deeper light enkindle, but for one, and one alone,

And that one myself, Beloved! — Oh my tender, calm and strong,
Oh to thee, my joy, my darling, do I consecrate this song!

Thou unknown and yet familiar, with what fervent prayers and tears
Have I sought thy fleeting image through the weary, endless years!

Sometimes heart and pulses thrilling, fancied for
    a little space
That I caught here, there, and yonder, glimpses
    of thy form and face;

But deceived, deluded ever, in the fond, sweet,
    foolish trust,
At my trembling touch the image crumbled into
    common dust!

Yet for all the hopeless yearning that was ever
    my sore part,
God's dear mercy never suffered that I gave my
    wayward heart

Unto any less of stature, smaller state or mould
    more mean
Than in thee I love and worship, O my royal
    Love unseen!

God's sweet mercy, that has kept me whole
    and pure and true for thee,
Even as thou, Love, 'neath the starlight, or beyond
    it, wait'st for me,

Somewhere, somewhere! — And though weary worlds divide us for a while,
Sometimes we shall clasp each other, speechless, with a silent smile,

Read the love through tears of rapture, that since life began we bore
Each to each, O my Beloved, — found, mine own forevermore!

O FLOWER MOST FINE!

O FLOWER most fine of Love Divine,
That to my soul had given
For bliss not found on earth's wide round
A joy of heaven, —

O source of song! that bright and strong
Once flashed beneath the sky,
Or like a brook in shady nook
Went murmuring by;

Turned in its flow to music low
The day's monotony,
While where it sang, luxurious sprang
Grass, flower, and tree;

White lilies fair that filled the air
With fragrance passing sweet,
'Neath the green shade where down I laid
Life's toil and heat. —

Through what dark power, in evil hour,
Did then thy founts run dry;
Through what sharp blight, in starless night,
Thy blossoms die?

Deep at the core where hope is o'er,
Shall this dark death be found? —
Or shall the source that in its course
Flowed underground

For a brief space, in power and grace
Leap forth once more to day,
From the brown root new blossoms shoot,
More fair than aye?

O Love Divine, the answer Thine
Unto the soul to give,
That as it fall must at Thy call
Perish or live!

GREECE.

I.

O MAGIC land, with sunny seas girt round,
And gentle hill-tops, whose dark forests shine
In the deep flush of morns and eves divine,
Thou who didst once with rapturous songs resound,
In the glad time when on thy shores was found
A happier people, flower most proud and fine
Of all our race, who drained the golden wine
Of beauty from a cup with roses crowned —
Wherefore turn we, whose brightest splendors seem
Of the full glory thine so long ago
But a faint echo, a pale after-gleam,
With love so great to thee that in its glow
Two thousand years of shadow melt away,
And thou arisest fair as yesterday?

II.

For oh, in thee the image we behold
Of that fresh, dew-gemmed morning, when the lyre
Still had unbroken music to inspire
The leaping blood with ecstasies untold,
Whose generous heat through weary years grew cold;
When it seemed easy task to snatch the fire
From heaven on high, with hands that could not tire,
Ere yet the saddened soul was wise and old;
Symbol of that proud power of early days,
When all things great were hoped and dared and done,
Which breathes in living stone or deathless lays
Of what no more shall come 'neath this pale sun —
That youth immortal that from age to age
Is still the world's most priceless heritage!

LIKE TO A BROOK, O SONG!

Too long, too long,
O my immortal song!
Like to a brook whose joyous life has lain
Fettered and hushed in winter's icy chain,
Wast thou imprisoned in my silent heart!
Now like that brook in Spring,
When the warm beam makes leaves and blos-
    soms start,
And joyfully the woods and valleys ring
With new-found lays of warblers on the wing,—
Unbound from ice and snow,
That do but help to swell thy flood and flow,
Of every trammel free,
Leap forth into the sun,
Thy new glad course begun
In fuller strength than yet was granted thee!

Flow on, flow on!
From twilight unto dawn,

Through morn and noon, and 'neath the star's
　　　pale glow,
And singing tell of all things thou shalt know!
— Of the fair child who bathes his dimpled feet,
Laughing aloud with glee,
In thy bright stream, or sails his tiny fleet,
— Of the fair maid, who bending down shall see
Her own sweet, blushing image glassed in thee,
— Of the glad even-tide,
When happy lovers walk thy banks beside,
Whispering in voices low,
Hand clasped in clinging hand,
Or in glad silence stand,
Amid the trees and flowers that round thee blow.

Away, away!
Thou canst not ever stay
'Mid this sweet peace, where thy small heart is
　　　stirred
By sun and shade, and flower and chant of bird,
But must from out thy pleasant fields haste down
Into the broader plain,
Past shimmering cities, and the populous town
Filled with the busy hum of toil and gain,
Whence shadows dim and sad thy brightness
　　　stain,

Where to thy waves shall flee
Fair innocence to save her purity,
Or sin and crime in dread
Haste their dark deeds to hide
In thy unruffled tide,
Where stately ships float near the silent dead.

So long, so long,
O my immortal song!
Till like that river thou hast seen and told
The deepest secrets that our lives may hold,
Flow ever on! — and like that river, fed
By springs unceasingly,
Grow still more wide thy banks, more deep thy
      bed,
Gather still fuller strength and majesty
On all thy course, yet mingle lavishly
Sweetness with power, so they
That drink of thee, refreshed go on their way.
And as unto the sea
That river hastes for aye, —
O my proud song, thus may
Thy currents all set to eternity!

BE STILL.

O joy! O happiness! since earliest days,
   Through many silent years,
I've waited for thee long and patiently,
   Prayed for thee with hot tears,
Sought thee 'neath many forms, on hundred paths
   Followed thee long and fleet,
Like to some eager boy, who does pursue
   With swift, untiring feet,
From dewy morn till noon — till the gray eve —
   Through vales, o'er hill-tops high,
O'er dusty highways, through green, flowery
     meads,
   Some golden butterfly,
That charms his sight and soul and lures him on,
   E'er on, resistlessly;
Now poising on some trembling lily-stem,
   Now on some small, brave tree
That spreads its crimson roses to the sun,
   And then perchance upon
The very path before him, at his feet,
   Yet ever and anon,

As he draws nigh, and with all eager hands,
  Fancies that he must clasp
The delicate wings that softly ope and close,
  Eluding his swift grasp,
And mockingly winging its flight away,
  E'er on and on again,
Till weary, breathless, he must pause at last,
  All his great hope grown vain!
Wherefore this be, I know not, O my soul,
  And may not answer thee!
Were it perchance that this frail, beauteous thing
  Is wrought so tenderly,
Captured, its life endured but one brief hour?
  Or that its delicate mould
Viewed closer by were not so passing fair?
  Or that the pallid gold
Which paints its splendor on the shimmering wings,
  Were bruised and paled away;
Turned to gray dust at the first touch of aught
  Fashioned of coarser clay?
I may not say nor question more; but know
  'T was thus my Father's will,
And that it is my part to rest content,
  And bid my heart be still!

ALL FUTURE YEARS ALONG.

THOU who hast been to me in by-gone years,
   For the great love that then was mine for thee,
The all-abundant source of bitter tears, —
   A spring whose waters flowed so lavishly,

So deeply mingled with a subtle bane,
   That those green days, when hope was young and bright,
And life had like a shimmering garden lain,
   Flooded with sun, in my enchanted sight,

All the wide spring-time landscape clouded hung
   As with the gray mists of perpetual rain,
The thousand beauteous blossoms there had sprung,
   Struck by a sudden cruel blight were slain,

Wilted and drooped, as touched by breath of fire,
   Till of all joys of gladsome earth was left
Not one my soul yearned toward with fond desire,
   Of that delight untold, thy love, bereft, —

Be to me still all future years along,
   For the great love is ever mine for thee,
The never-failing fount of sweetest song;
   A well shall spend its streams so generously,

So strong with secret, blest, life-giving power,
   That those sere days when hope is old and gray,
When, in the course of nature, leaf and flower
   Are stripped of brightness, droop and fade away,

The whole wide autumn landscape shall be clad
   In all the thousand charms of spring again,
All the parched, tender plants, newborn and glad,
   As with the freshness of soft summer rain,

After long drouth, — lift up their heads once more,
   Put forth new buds and blossoms passing fair,

That shall like incense delicate odor pour
   All round about them on the sunny air, —

A perfume so most strong, and sweet, and pure,
   That through unnumbered ages yet to be,
Within the souls of men shall still endure
   Our fragrant, undivided memory.

ABOVE AND EARTH AND TIME.

O LARK! that risest from dew-glistening fields
Into the cloudless, sun-filled morning sky,
Lost in the rapture of thy warbling song,
— Soaring so far, so high,
The earth with all its towering hills appears
But a green island in a wide, blue sea, —
What are to thee
The voices of the children in the field
That laugh and crow
So deep below,
The feeblest echo of their loudest glee
Scarce reaches thee? —

O soul! that risest from the happy earth
Into the boundless space of heaven on high,
Heedless if it be day or darksome night, —
— Soaring to God so nigh,
The world with all its petty cares, appears
But a dark speck in a vast sea of light, —

— That with unruffled calm dost contemplate,
And life and death, or good or evil fate,
That knowest thine the peace unspeakable,
Where tears and smiles are done,
And pain and joy as one, —
What were to thee the noisy voice of fame
Wherewith men chose perchance to herald thee,
Through every land and clime, —
Thee, that dost rise above and earth and time? —

IN VAIN.

In vain, O Life and Time! in vain
Your toil and strife, the end to gain
  Whereon your hearts are set!
Nor strength nor cunning shall avail,
Your wiliest efforts all must fail,
  To make my soul forget!

One working with the voiceless power
That silently saps rock and tower,
  Till there must sink away
The proudest spires that rise on high,
The cliffs that heaven's fierce storms defy,
  To dust and dark decay.

The other with the thunder's roar,
As when the waters to their core
  Cleaves the red lightning's sheen,
And right and left on either side
Rears in the flash the plunging tide
  Steep walls of quivering green.

One steady like a stream, whose strong
Yet gentle current bears along
  All darkness of the past,
On whose still shores the barren graves
Grow bright with flowers, whose water laves
  And heals all wounds at last.

One fitful as when northern nights
Are all aflame with flickering lights,
  Would charm with thousand strange
Fantastic forms of dazzling play
All memories from the heart away,
  In ceaseless whirl and change.

Greater than all things, save alone
And God and love and death, I own
  Your wondrous power, and yet
Shall all your toil and strife prove vain,
O Life and Time, that end to gain,
  To make my soul forget!

For when the goal seems well-nigh won,
Shall all your labor be undone,
  The dead shake off their pall;
In but thy smallest span, O Time,
The slightest of the gifts sublime,
  Thou, Life, must grant to all!

IN VAIN.

A gleam of moonlight on the sea,
A chance sweet strain of melody,
   The odor of a flower,
Would bring his image back with tears,
Through dust and death of thousand years,
   In all its undimmed power, —

Wake all those memories of yore
For evermore and evermore
   Mingled with joy and smart,
That even when my soul afar
Rejoicing floats from star to star,
   Must shake my inmost heart.

ETERNAL SPRING.

Deep in the dimmest recess of my soul,
   Faint as the passing fair
But yet scarce scented breath of spring that stole
   Into the wintry air;

Bound as the folded bud that shut from sight
   Beneath the hard, brown bark,
Giving no hint of the rich blossoms' white,
   Still slumbers in the dark;

Dumb as the unborn bird that in his shell,
   Wrapped in unconscious hush,
Dreams not the chant that from the living well
   Of his small throat shall gush, —

There lies the promise of a coming song,
   Unquickened, cold, and still,
While yet its heart in secret waxes strong,
   The fluttering pulses thrill.

And when the moment comes, the magic word
  Which the dark spell must break,
When balmy breath and bud and warbling bird
  To sudden life awake,

Then with such deathless power my song shall roll,
  With such deep sweetness ring,
That in the dimmest recess of my soul
  'T will make eternal spring!

SONNET.

From out the finest flower, the rich and strong
Most precious wine of deepest life, set free
By the deft touch of some rare alchemy,
We, though poor grasses of the field among,
Distill the golden honey of our song,
Ourselves in one, — O marvelous thing! — the bee
And fragrant blossom too. — But yet, ah me!
How in this whirling age, that spins along
On lightning's borrowed wings through space and time,
Shall such sweet, silent miracle be wrought? —
Never! — save when it may be as we climb
With daring feet those dizzy heights of thought,
We catch beyond dim midnight sun or star
A vision of the Godhead from afar!

TRANSFORMATION.

"Give me the wine of happiness," I cried,
"The bread of life! — O ye benign, unknown,
Immortal powers! — I crave them for my own;
I am athirst, I will not be denied
Though Hell were up in arms!" — No sound replied;
But turning back to my rude board and lone,
My soul, confounded, there beheld — a stone,
Pale water in a shallow cup beside!
With gushing tears, in utter hopelessness,
I stood and gazed. Then rose a voice that spoke, —
"God gave this, too, and what He gives will bless!"
And 'neath the hands that trembling took and broke,
Lo, truly a sweet miracle divine,
The stone turned bread, the water ruby wine!

SONNET.

The hour before the dawn; and all around
O'er heaven and earth and ocean far and nigh,
Stillness, in whose deep bosom every sigh
And breath of life, each faintest, fluttering sound
Seems hushed forever. Stillness so profound
I know not if it gently floats on high
Out of my heart, or from the star-filled sky
Descends, a benediction earthward bound.
But in that heart from tears and sorrow free,
There slowly rises — as on some dark sea
A lily flower with richest perfume fraught,
Its glimmering petals to the night unfurled
That folds it lovingly — the blessed thought:
The Peace of God has come into the world!

SONNETS.

SOLITUDE.

I LOVE thee, O thou Beautiful and Strong,
  Invisible comrade, mute, sweet company,
  More dear than friend or lover! But to thee
My fondest hopes, my fairest dreams belong
For evermore! Amid the world's gay throng
  I yearn for thy soft arms that lovingly
  Soothe all the fevered wounds once fretting me.
At thy deep heart there springs the fount of song
Whose drops shall cool my burning lips athirst, —
  At thy swift beck within my sight arise
(Their bonds of silence and dim darkness burst)
  All my beloved dead, with shining eyes, —
  At thy blest hand, by starlit paths untrod,
  My soul draws near unto the face of God!

SILENCE.

Ay, and thee, too, who wield'st a power divine,
  Greater than loudest speech or fairest lay!
  The dead, millions on millions, own thy sway,
In realms where suns, to rise no more, decline.
Thine is the lover's sweetest rapture, thine
  The deepest cup of grief or joy, that aye
  The lips of mortal tasted; thine — yet stay —
How may I name thee, with what sound so fine
It shall not snap thy life's frail, golden thread?
  O Solitude and Silence, bid me learn
A little of your greatness! Long are fled
  The lesser gods of life, now let me turn
  To ye alone, to ye in worship come,
    The accents of this faltering tongue grown dumb!

SONNET.

From out eternal silence do we come;
Into eternal silence do we go;
For was there not a time, and swift or slow,
Must come again, when all this world's loud hum
Was naught to us, and must again grow dumb
Through all eternity? — Between two low,
Dark, stony portals, with much empty show
Of tinkling brass and sounding fife and drum,
The endless Caravan of Life moves on;
Or whence or whither, to what destiny,
But He who dwells beyond the furthest dawn
Knows, yet reveals not, evermore even He
In silence wrapt, though deepest thunders roll,
Save for His deathless message to our soul!

www.ingramcontent.com/pod-product-compliance
Lightning Source LLC
Chambersburg PA
CBHW030343170426
43202CB00010B/1222